Hymns for Unaccompanied Trumpet

by William Bay

ISBN 978-098-883-275-6

WILLIAM
BAY MUSIC

Visit us on the Web at www.williambaymusic.com

Preface

The trumpet is a brilliant instrument which shines brightly when playing proclamatory pieces. However, the trumpet also has a wonderfully lyrical side. The sound of an unaccompanied trumpet causes people to take note. It is a sound that announces something to come, or as the case may be, a poignant memory of what has gone before.

I wrote the enclosed 54 arrangements and compositions to capture the beauty of solo, unaccompanied trumpet. Two of the selections are written for two trumpets. Some are well known hymns and some are lesser known lyrical pieces from early American hymnody. There are ancient chants and an original communion setting called *The Lord's Supper*.

I hope you enjoy performing these pieces as much as I did in writing them.

William Bay

Contents

Abide With Me
Eventide

Andante ♩ = 86

William Henry Monk
arr. by William Bay

Doxology #1

Louis Bourgeois
arr. by William Bay

Adoro Devote

Gently ♩ = 74

13th Century Plainsong
arr. by William Bay

6

Doxology #2
Geistliche Kirchengesänge

arr. by William Bay

♩ = 94 **A**

B

rit.

7

Am I Born To Die?
Idumea

Slowly ♩ = 88

Sacred Harp, 1835
arr. by William Bay

8

rit.

36

For the Beauty of the Earth
Dix

Conrad Kocher
arr. by William Bay

♩ = 90

A

mf

6

B

12

17

22

Be Thou My Vision
Slane

Irish Melody
arr. by William Bay

Moderately ♩ = 104

Beneath the Cross of Jesus
St. Christopher

Frederick C. Maker
arr. by William Bay

Moderately ♩ = 88

Bread of the World
Eucharistic Hymn

Gently ♩ = 86

John S. B. Hodges, 1868
arr. by William Bay

Christ Be in My Heart
Bi a ´losa im Chroise

Trad. Irish
arr. by William Bay.

Slowly ♩ = 82

Come Ye Sinners, Poor and Wretched
Beach Spring

Sacred Harp, 1835
arr. by William Bay

14

Come, Holy Spirit
Abbeville

From the Sacred Harp, 1844
arr. by William Bay

Moderately ♩ = 90

mf

Come, Thou Fount of Every Blessing
Nettleton

Lively ♩ = 100

Wyeth's Repository of Sacred Music, 1813
arr. by William Bay

A

B

Love Divine
Beecher

John Zundel
arr. by William Bay

♩ = 100

Easter Fanfare
For Two Trumpets

Boldly ♩ = 96

William Bay

O God, Unseen Yet Ever Near
St. Flavian

Communion Hymn

arr. by William Bay

Fairest Lord Jesus
St. Elizabeth

Lyrically ♩ = 94

arr. by William Bay

Amazing Grace

John Newton

arr. by William Bay

Swing Feeling

♩ = 92   **A**

21

Glory Be to Jesus
Caswall

Friedrich Filitz, 1847
arr. by William Bay

Moderately ♩ = 84

22

Guide Me, O Thou Great Jehovah
CWM Rhondda

Majestically ♩ = 92

John Hughes
arr. by William Bay

Here, O My Lord, I See Thee Face to Face
Penitentia

Lyrically ♩ = 84

Edward Dearle
arr. by William Bay

24

Holy, Holy, Holy
Nicaea

John B. Dykes, 1861
arr. by William Bay

Boldly ♩ = 88

I Will Arise and Go to Jesus
Arise/Restoration

Gently ♩ = 84

Southern Harmony, 1835
arr. by William Bay

Jesus Calls Us
Pleading Savior

Early American Hymn
arr. by William Bay

It is Well With My Soul
Ville Du Havre

Philip P. Bliss 1838-1876
arr. by William Bay

Lyrically ♩ = 92

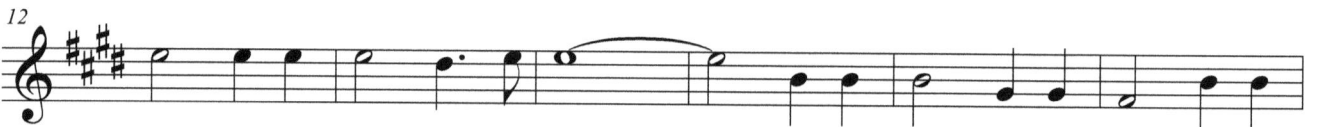

Breathe on Me, Breath of God
Trentham

Robert Jackson
arr. by William Bay

Let All Mortal Flesh Keep Silence
Picardy

Trad. French
arr. by William Bay

Gently ♩ = 74

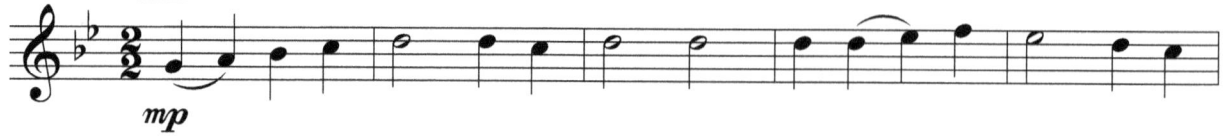

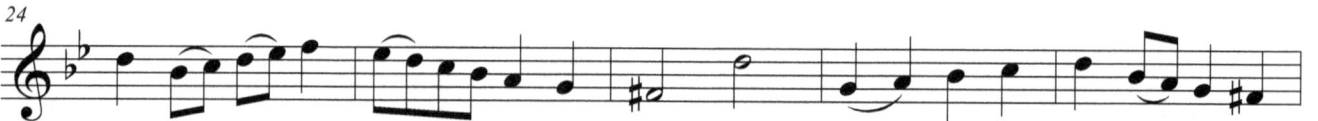

Lord, Speak to Me
Canonbury

Robert Schumann
arr. by William Bay

31

O God, We Praise Thee
Morning Song

Gently ♩ = 82

Early American Sacred Song
William Bay

Come, Holy Ghost
Veni Creator

Sarum Plainsong, Mode VIII
arr. by Willilam Bay

O Savior, Rend the Heavens Wide
O Heiland, Reiss Die Himmel Auf

Boldly ♩ = 100

Gesangbuch, Augsburg, 1666
arr. by William Bay

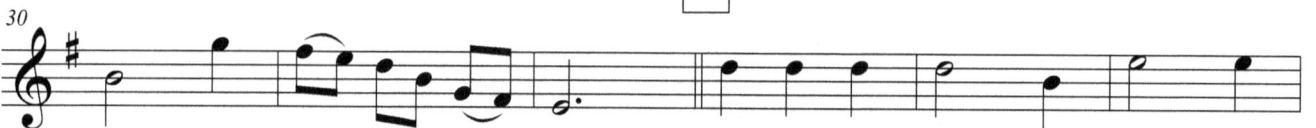

Palmetto
Trumpet Duet

Early American Hymn, 186:

William Bay

Adagio ♩ = 66

35

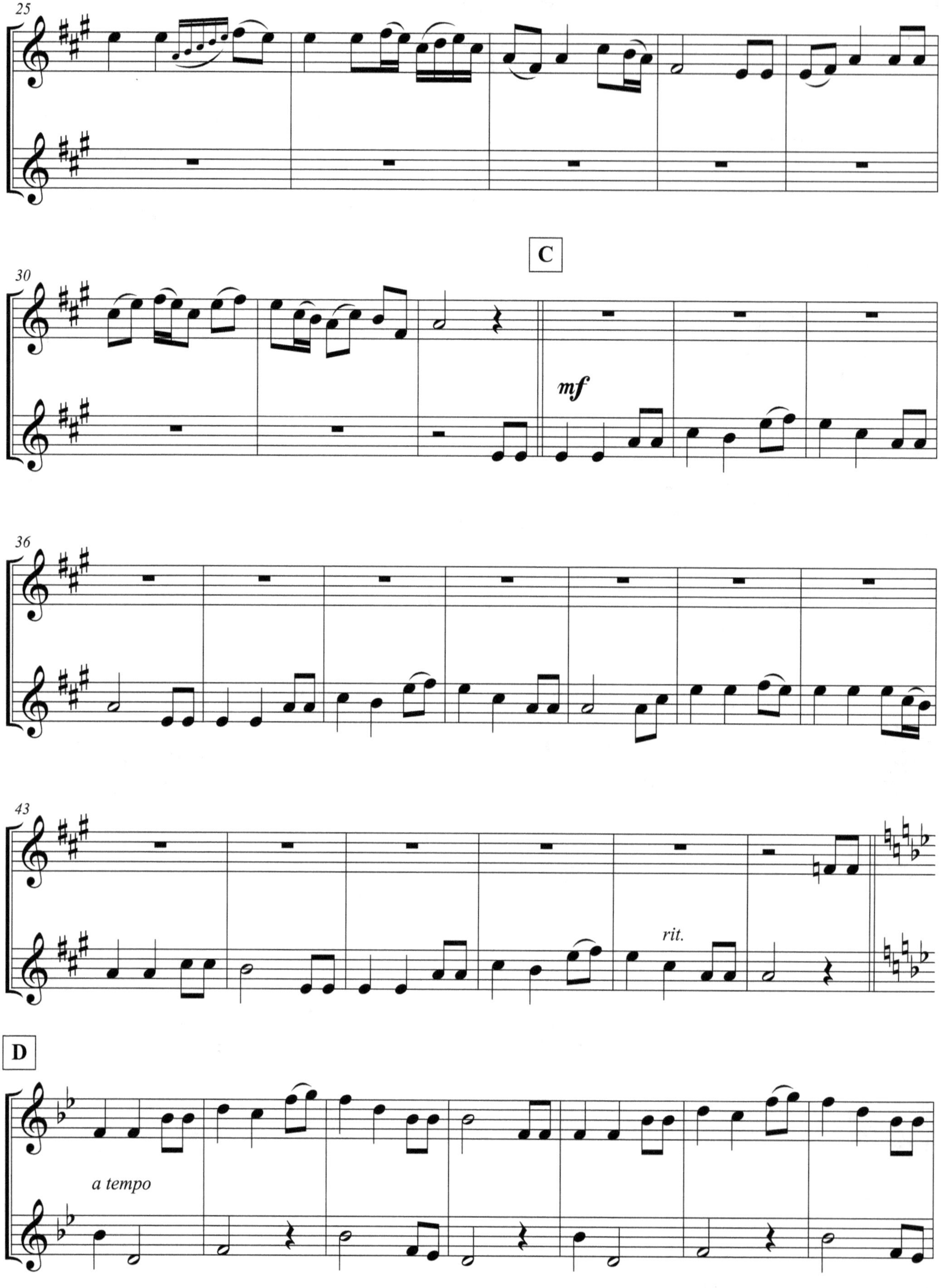
25
C
30
mf
36
43
rit.
D
a tempo

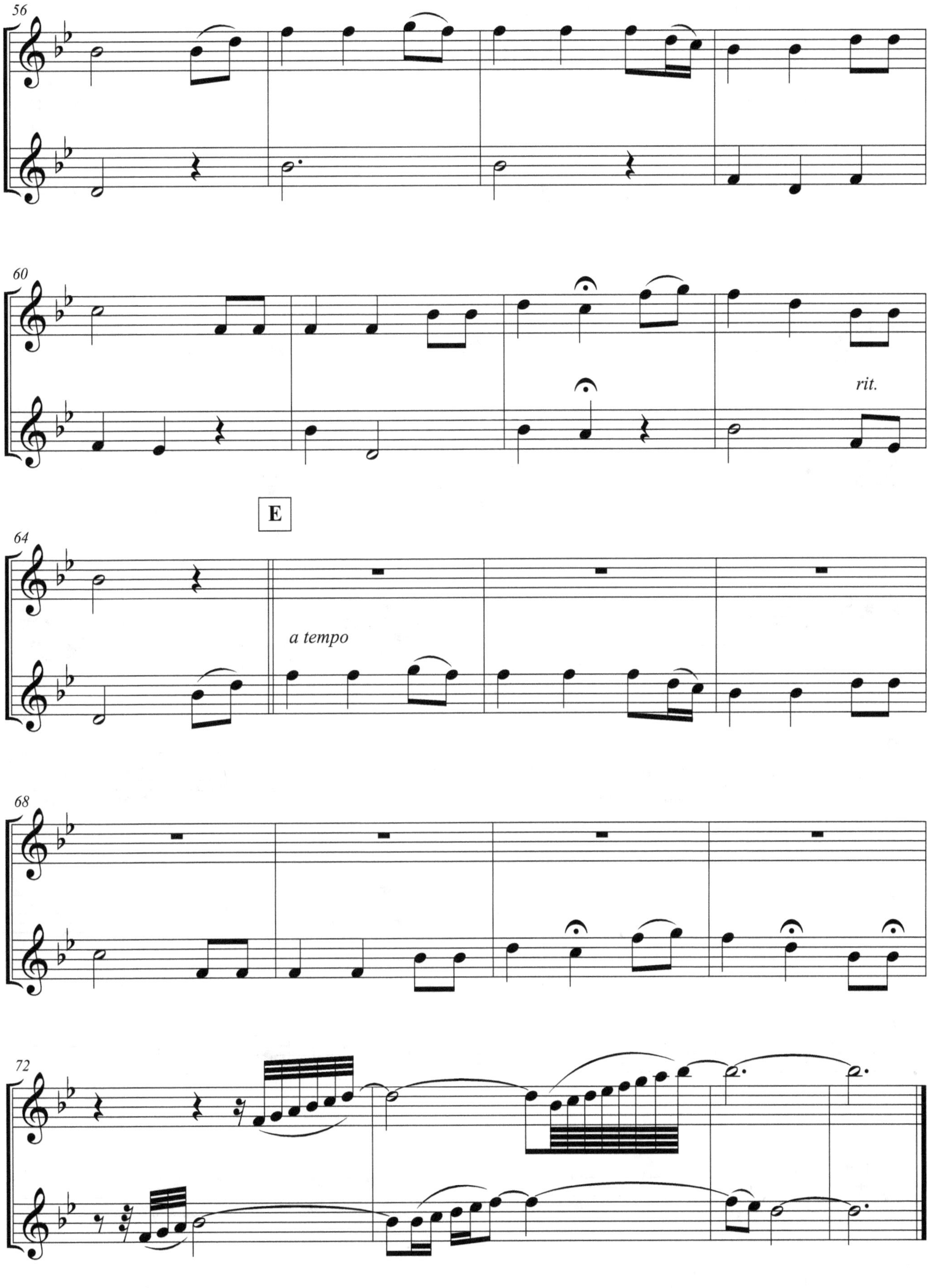
56
60
rit.
E
64
a tempo
68
72

Praise My Soul, The King of Heaven
Lauda Anima

Boldly ♩ = 96

John Goss, 1869
arr. by William Bay

Praise to the Lord, the Almighty
Lobe den Herren

Boldly ♩ = 110

Joachim Neander
arr. by William Bay

Trumpet in B♭

39

Rejoice, The Lord is King
Darwall

Boldly ♩ = 110

John Darwall
arr. by William Bay

Shall We Gather at the River
Hanson Place

Robert Lowry
arr. by William Bay

Reverently ♩ = 84

41

Shall We Gather/Alternate
Palmetto

Early American Hymn, 1865
arr. by William Bay

Adagio ♩ = 66

Thaxted

Gustav Holst
arr. by William Bay

Boldly ♩ = 96

A

mf

6

13

B

20

mf

27

34

41

C *Slower*   *rit.*

48

43

The Church's One Foundation
Aurelia

Moderately ♩ = 82

Samuel Wesley
arr. by William Bay

This Day is Past and Gone
Evening Shade

Moderato ♩ = 120

Sacred Harp, 1835
arr. by William Bay

The God of Abraham Praise
Leoni

Meyer Lyon
arr. by William Bay

Moderately ♩ = 108

The King of Love My Shepherd Is
St. Columba

Lyrically ♩ = 90

Traditional Irish
arr. by William Bay

47

The Lord is My Shepherd
Brother James' Air

J.L.Macbeth Bain
arr. by William Bay

Gently

A

B

C

The Lord's My Shepherd
Crimond

Moderate tempo ♩ = 92

Jessie Seymour Irvine
arr. by William Bay

The Lord's Supper

Gently ♩ = 92

William Bay

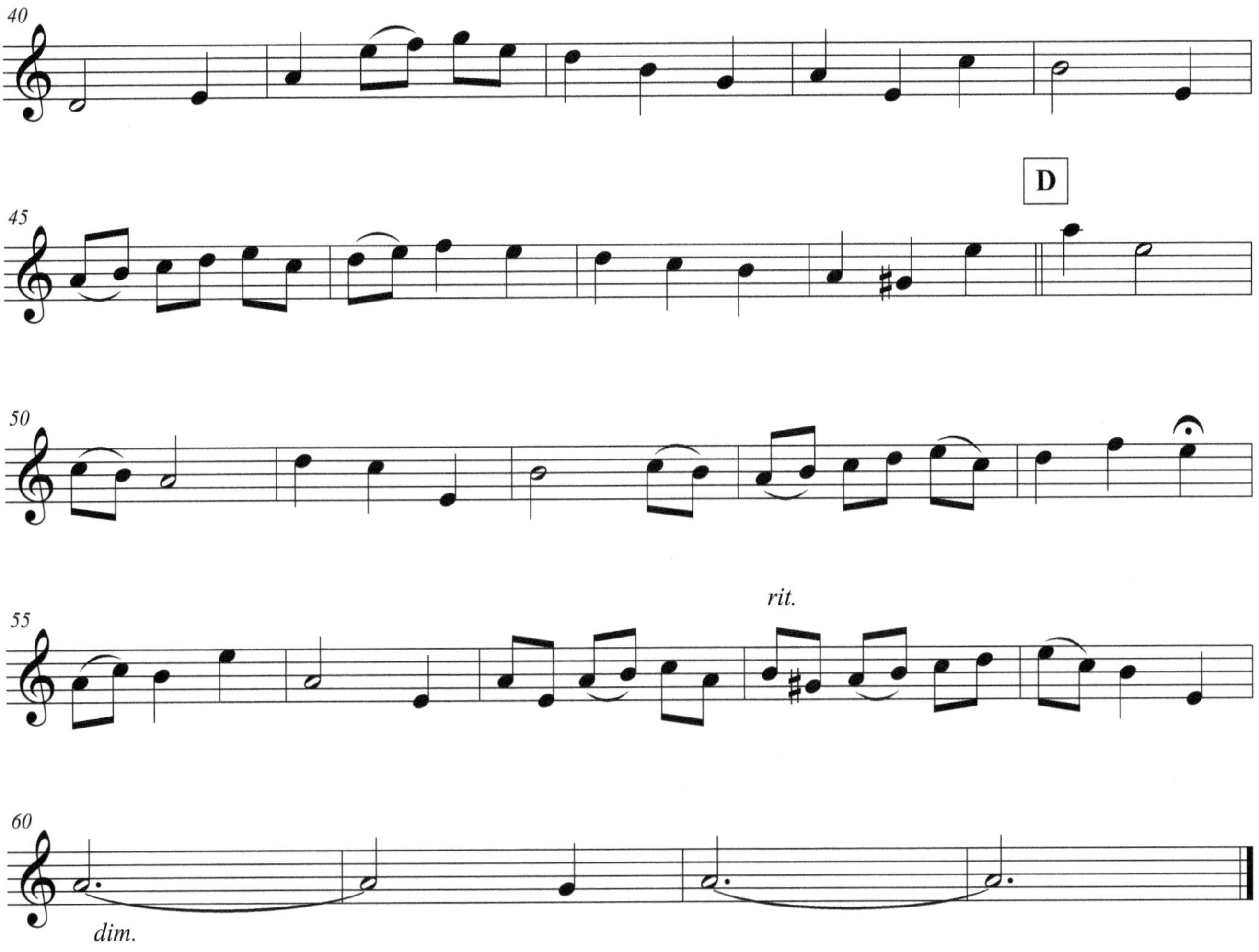
40
45
D
50
55
rit.
60
dim.

The Wedding Feast of Cana
Ag an bPósadh Bhi i gCána

Trad. Irish
arr. by William Bay

Wayfarin' Stranger
Spiritual

arr. by William Bay

Veni Redemptor gentium

Gently ♩ = 86

Plainsong, 12th Century

arr. by William Bay

54

Doxology #3
Tallis Canon

Thomas Tallis
arr. by William Bay

We Gather Together to Ask the Lord's Blessing
Kremser

Moderately ♩ = 98

Nederlandtsch Gedenckclank, 1626
arr. by William Bay

When I Survey the Wondrous Cross
Rockingham

Isaac Watts
arr. by William Bay

Moderately ♩ = 96

When Jesus Left His Father's Throne
Kingsfold

Boldly ♩ = 104

Traditional English
arr. by William Bay

A

B

C

Now Thank We All Our God
Nun Danket

Johann Crüger
arr. by William Bay

A Mighty Fortress Is Our God
Ein' Feste Burg

Martin Luther
arr. by William Bay

www.ingramcontent.com/pod-product-compliance
Lightning Source LLC
Chambersburg PA
CBHW050452110426

42744CB00013B/1973